M000294698

Also by Michael S. Weaver

POETRY
Water Song, *1985*
Signatures #3, *1985* (pamphlet)
My Father's Geography, *1992*

CHAPBOOK
some days it's a slow walk to evening, *1989*

Stations in a Dream

by

Michael S. Weaver

Dolphin-Moon Press and Lite Circle Books
Baltimore

The author wishes to gratefully acknowledge James Taylor for all he has done to help him sustain him in his belief.

The publishers wish to acknowledge a number of publications for the following poems appearing in this collection: "Bathsheba," "David," "The Falling Angel," and "The Praying Jew" in *Obsidian II;* "Solitude" and "Lovers With Flowers" in *Hudson River;* "The Falling Angel" in **Free State: A Harvest of Maryland Poets** (SCOP Publications); "Purim" and "Jew at Prayer" in *Maryland Poetry Review;* and "Peasant Life" and "Lovers Under Lilies" in *The Gleaner*.

ISBN 0-940475-01-4
Copyright 1993 Dolphin-Moon Press and The Lite Circle, Inc.

The publishers wish to recognize the assistance of the National Endowment for the Arts, the Maryland State Arts Council, and the Baltimore Mayor's Advisory Committee on Art and Culture.

Cover art: Aissatou Mijiza
Back cover photograph: Michael Bergman
Special thanks to Rebecca Sleeme and Michele Williams for proofreading and to Nicholas Wm. Aumiller for cover pre-mechanicals.

Dolphin-Moon Press
P.O. Box 22262
Baltimore, MD 21203

Lite Circle Books
P.O. Box 26162
Baltimore, MD 21210

Dolphin-Moon Press is an independent publisher dedicated to excellence and invention in the arts. If you are interested in these goals, please request our free catalog.

Lite Circle Books is a division of The Lite Circle, Inc., a non-profit literary association devoted to the encouragement of emerging voices in the arts. Please write for more information.

This collection of poems is
lovingly dedicated
to
Aissatou Mijiza

These poems were inspired by the oeuvre of Marc Chagall, the great Russian-Jewish painter who was born Moyshe Shagal to followers of Baal Shem Tov in 1887 in Pestkovatik. Not a member of any artistic school, Monsieur Chagall lived for most of his life in France, where he died in 1985 in Vence.

Contents

Love Among the Living

Love in the Word

Love Among the Living

The Tree of Life

On the day we married, wholeness reigned,
music sprang from the full bud of a man
like a flower flying above the synagogue,
a presumptuous rooster pranced in the clouds;
the tree of life arose in its perfection
as large and beckoning as the sun, and
miracles worked their small fingers
in our ears, tickling and becoming;
wishes we made as children turned incarnate,
the fruit of the trees was succulent,
not false or admonishing, and we were filled
with the sudden light like vessels crafted
by nimble hands just for that second.
We tasted wisdom and it has enriched us,
fed our hearts to bursting, set our souls
to dancing on the strings that bind the dream.

Adam and Eve

The serpent had an agent,
a tiny stag with a bird perched
on antlers that shone like silver,
suggesting flight to Eve, soaring
above the tree with its blue leaves,
going into the giant bass of God.
Adam was proud of his wife and the tree,
admiring the gesticulating trunk,
laughing at the snake's ludicrous dancing
like a drunken emperor. Before the fruit,
they held knowledge suspect,
but had no warning of the truth-
of life's prescience and power to transform.
Eve wept at the beauty of the faces in shadows.

Bride with Fan

With each petal to this fan,
tie my heart to morning windows
with fresh cut flowers from
my garden, and a lock of his hair.

Tie them also to a daughter
who knows music and the stars,
can throw trills at Orion,
and prime my tears with her soprano.

Tie them to my death, Lord,
so only the virtuous will bury me,
and nothing hard be said of this fan.

The Wedding

Should I promise you something,
right here while you hold my hand
and the cock crows and the goat pokes
his head through the crowd, laughing?

Should I tell you something no one else
shall ever hear, not even when secrets
are revealed, when tears are shed communally,
when bent heads amble up the roads?

Should I give you a touch somewhere
that will never be replicated, only enjoyed
in memory in our private recounting,
when youth slips away and eternity beckons?

Should I take you from this festive crowd
with a kiss that suddenly reveals the world
above, the contemplative ascent through
the heavens to bliss, as we wed and close circles?

Bathsheba

Not even white dresses, fresh blossoms
or the despairing angels hovering could change
the fire that seized you the night after
she was through her period and her womb
lay open and fertile, beckoning you,
arousing you, leading like a siren.

Not all the concubines combined could deter
the beckoning of history, not even the memory
of how Michal saved your life could break the trance
of Bathsheba as you saw her bathing and allowed lust
to set your breath and soul on fire,
until there could be no euphony but your body with hers

emitting the percussion and wail of passion,
until you could have her beneath you, her eyes
widened and brightened by your driving sin.
And when death seemed the answer, you dispatched
it with all the authority of God's king,
all the madness and delirium of greed and guilt.

You chose your love from forbidden quarters,
and Solomon's soul sang in the marrow of your bones.

David

In your old age you adored the lyre.
All the women and all the births
were one wavering image, your trembling body
kept warm by a beautful girl
you could only turn your eyes to and smile,
caress with the weak hands of a father.

A boy's ambitions can end in dreaming,
or they can be applauded by God
and given the power of metamorphosis,
changing like the angelic host from
wisp and mist to flesh, blood, stone,
wood, and fire — to life's stock.

You looked at Abishag, at her unblemished
figure, the soft call of her curling lips,
the dark hair falling on your shoulder
as she massaged your rigid neck
and rubbed her thighs against yours
to keep the king immortal, but desire was gone.

You remembered the countless marriages, the children,
wondered, without love, how could you have dreamed.

Bouquet with Flying Lovers

Let's not go in, just yet, while the night
is hanging full and we have the power of air,
above the village's soft noise, and
the loud audacity of the bouquet.

Let's not give up the power of lovemaking,
the transcendental and metamorphic power
of perspiring skin and joining tongues,
and the shudder of orgasm thrusting us out.

We have become apparitions in dreams
baking in the heads of snoring old men,
hosts in the fantasies alive in the slumber
of young women spread in their sheets.

This is not a momentary splendor,
but flight eternal if we will just hover a while,
and connect with the stars' immutability,
become burning fixtures in the night, for desire.

The Three Candles

For our consummation tonight,
we will leave behind the petty lights,
show oblivious eyes to the gaping faces,
shut our ears to the patient violin's pace.

Shout in my year so I can hear the wild
beating of my own heart above the clamor piled
beneath us from the jester with his horn,
and the gathered neighbors laughing but forlorn.

Our nuptial bed is being prepared
by angelic hands that rushed and dared
presume the temple reparable, encased the hearts
of the rabbis with the Siddur's art.

And in it we will celebrate our nakedness and bonding
by the unabashed revealing of heaven's play,
the hosts applauding, lighting the heart's three fires,
showing the blessed light of desire.

Lovers with Flowers

Can you contain my most intimate whisper,
settle it down after it has entered you,
make it a part of you and still cling
to my hand as gently as your eyes hold me?

Something must protect our weakness,
our mortality, and I choose the petal
and the leaf for their own transcience,
as life is emboldened by mortal fear.

In this light through this glass and wood,
I sleep confidently in your murmurs and dreams,
deaf to significance, delighting
in our petty island of flowers and silences.

You have turned my soul to blazing pith.

The Dream

I am numb and naked from ecstasy.
My legs are parted and hung round
the neck of some obedient phantasm,
where they burn at the apex,
as my pelvis has been set aflame
by this journey to heaven, lovemaking
that removes me from earth
and sets me on the tiny clamor
of angels examining my nudity and dazed splendor.
Walking on stars, the earth hangs
its trees and patterned fields in my eyes;
moving mouths utter conversations minute
and inaudible, as I dream that
I can illumine the world with
my body naked and empowered by sex,
joining the moon in its white casting of light.

Russian Wedding

The fiddler played a personal tune,
something out of his love for dancing,
apart from the moment. Grandmother
crackled behind me, walking in prayer.
Gray and white frolicked in the sky,
threatening my life at windows,
crying into decorated cloth at the rain;
the fiddler lost himself in the strings;
children stopped and eyed my parade,
peering into the crowded world
of smiles and tears crawling over the hill,
the procession that would dare
grow to the size of an army and
the festive blurting of flower bazaars.
When the memory is old and near death,
when Grandmother whistles from cobwebs,
the fiddler strikes his strings alone.
Old man Elijah crosses with two pails of milk;
the hunger and the feeding must go on.

Birth

When I dream of your birth,
jesters in yellow costumes
press waxen smiles and hands
against the glass, pushing
to see if it will shatter and fly,
if they can stop your laughter.

Uncle Ezra always steps
out in his night clothes, alabaster
and crippled by the strings
that pull people in dreams,
that make this one full of red walls
under a ceiling mated with the sky.

When the crimson bird is served,
the spell will be broken, faces
contorted like evil masks will turn
to embroidered flowers on the wall,
my prayers will admit your soul,
this dream will die and release your birth.

David in Profile

He never wanted to understand
the plucked chords of a table
set with flowers in a room of red,
or the infantile gurgling of his own music.
I tried to bring him to that.

Sometimes waking, he would break away,
leave me alone and run out
in a meadow with his arms stretchèd
high until he tore his sleeves
and his naked back shone under
the shadows of tiny leaves on him
like the paws of an infinite monkey,
until he screamed, "This is love."

I am always advising my birds to surrender,
tending their cages in the morning,
tickling their breasts until they stand
in laughter that abides and conceals
the hate. I am always telling them,
in the soft conversation of the spiritual,
of the harshness of an unprotected life,
arguing the valid hope of my heart,

like a woman carefully preparing a room
for love.

The Birthday

Your heart and mine are too different,
one a bickering roustabout that lounges
in the company of old men,
the other a yellow prodigy
that flies dutifully into the sun.

As bouquets are for wishing,
I have turned my spine inside out,
brought you one despite my indulgence,
my preference for lewd songs and laughter,
obeying the omens I have ignored
all my life, my blessed life, my dogged life.

You are imperturbable, cruising to the sun,
believing once there you can touch me
with a finger flaming and aloft,
set the lattice of my brain aright,
bring me to your room to lie down
and join the carnival of the city,
be at ease with life's creak and groan.
I celebrate your birthday with consenting.

My whispers want you to know
we are getting on, the light is dimming,
the night sounds are only life letting life.

Peonies and Lilacs

In the peonies are two tiny figures,
a woman in white and a patient man
who holds her by the shoulders and sings,
songs from the old world long beyond us,
the world of Samuel and Esther,
eons before Russia with its pogroms;
he offers a drink distilled from
the perfume of stamens, lifting it
to her lips with hands as delicate
as lace, as old as the firmament,
and she parts her lips slowly, smiling;
minute and cheering laughter bubbles
from the lilacs around them,
and they are safe in the arms of my guze,
a life apart from snoozing neighbors.

The Spoonful of Milk

Stalking me from the stove,
she's easing another spoonful of milk,
spilling into my soaked beard,
sobbing about the virtue of warm milk
for the sleepless, those with pacts
drawn with the legion of spirits,
those with red eyes like painted eggs
and fatigue that turns to immobility.

Frightened by the evenings,
I have taken to reading novels,
fully dressed in my yellow cap,
hoping the words will take me
back into themselves, into
that soft world of nothing
that precedes the word, issuing
off the trail of God's breath,
hoping words will take me
to the sovereign state of dreams.

She's hunting me again
with another spoonful of milk;
I wait for the name of a foreign place
to take me with an inviting hand.

Mariaska

Light coalesced
in the butterflies,
formed minute webs
in the wings
caught in the line
of the sofa.
She begged
the flowers patiently,
eyes teeming
under the hat
blackened by green.
Her naked feet and legs
slid from under
her dress, explicating,
piercing the oppression
of jealousy filling
the room.
He never came.

Lovers under Lilies

The hungry throats of the lilies
let down transparent tongues
with tips licking at the nipples
of your breasts naked in the corner
of my arm, as round as moon faces;
your lips follow your surprise,
the shimmer that shouts your consent
from a voice in your eyes,
and I am lost in the thick road
of your black hair falling,
disappearing into its unnamed curves;
something inside me wants to leave me,
feeling desperately that it belongs to you
and to the primal tongues of the lilies.

Interior II

Before entering the labyrinth,
Ariadne admonished Theseus,
told him she knew of his drinking,
his boasting among the men.

Her scarf dangling about her head,
she grabbed his beard,
and fell soft and helpless
in his eyes, his putrid breath.

In their scrambling they broke the lamp,
the hollow darkness revealed
snorting and stomping in the distance,
intimations of a lover to be abjured.

The Violinist

Ruth and David stopped making love,
Ruth naked to the waist and waving,
her breasts like oranges or smiles;
they asked me to play another love song.
In the yellow curve of the path,
they threw coins at me and the boy,
birds mistaking them for bread and
attacking them from the roof in bursts,
shaming Ruth and David, who valued their money.
David covered himself with the scented towel,
but I saw their nakedness in my music,
whose memory is instant. At the point of creation,
it shoots backwards simultaneously,
through love's flesh to the eye of God.

Red Nude Sitting Up

I sit against the rocks under yellow moons,
light turns crimson all over me as I disrobe,
place my clothes on the limbs of a fir,
and let the pink breath of cherubs flush me.
The moon puts ovals around my nipples,
turns the soft arcs of my legs to hard angles,
darkens the hair of my vagina until
it is like a hole in the earth, going to the core
where the moon's jealousy is kept lit.

I smile at the square edge of my knee,
the ledge of abdomen where children lie waiting,
my breasts settling smoothly as I turn.

I am being filled with something, a song
is coming in the night wind of Shekhinah
and putting electric in my nerves like
the shooting of life in the green fuse.

Now I shall never know confusion.

Woman with a Bouquet

The gardener said I was mad for peacocks,
when I stuffed the vase with yellows,
blues, reds. The whole thing was aflame
with colors, bright illuminations that guided me home;
I bought them for their evocative power,
their ability to rouse the slumbering heart,
to remind old promises of themselves and
make them pound the soul into fidelity,
to take the feet and point them home.
Each spring I have done this ritual
to give myself Circe's power and Venus's endurance,
to call him back from the wandering.
I only pray my flowers are not idle displays,
that my soul is not Dido's dark kin.

Birth (1910)

The old men labored in the corner,
gesturing while the younger ones crowded
around whispers, studying the gestures
of their fingers upturned in the yellow light;
one argued the young girl's felicity in spring,
another did a slow swagger and dance,
expounding on the majestic ripple
of a young man's back cutting wood in autumn;
the white beard of a neighbor
moved in the window like a marionette,
straining to see through the red canopy
of the bed. Small birds swam over
the blood. The father hid under the bed;
the naked mother hung to
the one sheet thickened with her cries,
her full breasts tilted over the tub.
The midwife's red fingers concealed the gift.

Madonna of the Village

Each night that Christ is ushered to Earth
by the Madonna, her airy body clothed
in shimmering light like a bride's veil and gown,
a giant candle usurps the union of sun and moon.

The angels attend Mary and Christ like the raucous allies
of Ariel, falling from the great throne
down through the seven heavens, delighted
by the festive roll of trumpets in breaking clouds.

Gabriel flies down to push his lips on her brow,
ennunciating the holy body of the dream,
establishing another station where hope's possibilities
transcend the Oral Torah, as the village sleeps.

The red supplication of the violin turns
the heavenly court from awe to celebration;
principalities argue the text, the night swells,
the groom rushes to her heart with a bouquet.

Solitude

Alone I meditate on the invisible,
the potentially beautiful and minute chasms
of meaning that divide me and God,
the trailing words from his mouth
whose echoes taunt me with suggestions
of the Oral Torah, the grand perfection
before the first droplet of water,
or the setting of the first grain of sand.
Inside I listen for him to enter me,
to flow into this infinite cavern of my heart
and help me know this quiet village
behind me and the solitary angel above,
as other sanctities beg in my shadow,
offering foreign altars and hymns.

Love in the Word

Vitebsk

Watching the city from this root,
the trees are like the heads of an audience
waiting for the houses to play some drama,
to push out the characters from Verdi,
or Puccini, or something quiet and striking
in the heart like a Chekhovian world,
lifetimes of emotion reduced to seconds;
the globe is a genius unto itself,
suddenly replicating its own shadows
in the finitude of our minds imagining.
Watching the city from this root,
caught in the web of a tree's tie
to earth, the city is a dream adrift,
and I count the amazing eyes that travel.

Half Past Three

I trust the world with its metaphors,
each word possessing its own clock,
dictating to the smaller universes
that form the infinite networks of our hearts,
sounding the essential in the genteel clink of glass.

The cat puts his tongue of stubble on my elbow,
gently vibrating the shell of my bones,
while I lean on the red bar pouring wine
into my mind; in this superfluous minute
the world is primal, breathing in lines and circles.

The world multiplies and dominates,
other spheres imagine themselves and float,
spin out behind my inflamed head, spilling
flowers out of the copulation of mass and color;
still I trust the metaphors of multiple worlds

as well as I know the single personal one,
with its infinite apotheosis of words in my hand.

White Crucifixion

Such quiet peace on the face of death,
hands and feet impaled, blood choking
on itself, the patriarchs flying above,
announcing a prophecy's completion.
Wherever we flee, past the burning doors
of the temple, down summoning roads
with children in arms, falling out
of upturned houses, trampled by indolent feet
of revolutionaries touting their banners,
wherever life waxes murderous and unforgiving,
there is this music of a quiet death,
plucked by the elders and their angels
for a lifeless countenance bathed in the sacred
and imperturbable — God's insistent light.

The Praying Jew

Seven severe indications of my love for you
were in the wall, flaming like the aura
around the temple at Sinai, speaking
in voices ranging to the imperceptible,
the invisible soprano of hosannahs,
of manna falling like walls of rain at night,
and I awoke grasping for your embrace.

Walk with me past the dropping of the moon,
to where we inhabit the ocean and
our sojourn is through the cold timber
of my heart, to its center where you
can kiss it and set the world to beginning,
to creating and recreating itself infinitely,
to its center where I will vanish with you.

Hear my soul singing to you, shouting to me,
shimmering like the blinding vision of Ezekiel,
streaming down like the Oral Torah,
from your tongue to the Earth, to hearing.
Hear my soul reaching back to the full cloth
of your breath that rendered it to me.
Hear my prayer of desire for divine love.

Homage to Apollinaire

The magician caught in the stone,
frozen by rock's refusal to negotiate
movement in its stillness, allows
his head to turn enough to catch
two doves coasting by, or the shrieks
of the woman who holds him there,
meditating on the slumber of the world
and his sensuous power to awaken it,
to set all flesh to lovemaking,
to make midnight eternal and flowing,
to bind her heart with his, and
train her trills with the magic of dawn.
As he loosens the stone, freeing his blood,
she clutches her naked body, meditating louder,
afraid of the harmonizing wave of love's revenge.

Chrysanthemums

Gabriel reduces himself to the size of a wish
or the staggered laugh of an infant watching
the leaves blow and flip in the window
like the busy hands of dancers working round
like stems. He sails past us with a gentle hand
turned up to receive his ordination from
ancients relaxing among the Pleiades,
governing the motions of apparitions like those
who appeared to Lot in desperate Sodom;
his low and miniature cruising is affirmed
by the glimmer of nodding heads we must not see.
He studies the petals of the chrysanthemums,
slowly remembering earth, the tactile pleasure
of walking on soil and stone, and startled
by the old temptation of domains and regality,
he becomes a gasp and flies into the gold flower.

The Poet Reclining

I can never convince my father
that my best work is done in naps,
in the greenest of grass, near the smell
of manure, of the song of neighing
and snorting, in the infinite music
that fills the word with bright meaning.

After I am half out of life,
I can have discourse with the trees,
with each leaf that tickles itself,
and flirts with the branch, sending
me the secrets of a woman,
of the distinguishing flurry of her smile.

In this grass I always dream that
if I stay a little longer I will leave
this skin, skull, heart, brain,
femur, and blood, and melt into the soil
and multiply like the infinite beads
of this planet, becoming the thing
I spend my life singing to.

But I cannot convince my father,
who uses manure, tearfully, for flowers,
hoping to raise my mother
from her berth in the earth.

Self-Portrait

I see myself in the shadows of a leaf
compressed to the green blades growing
to a point like the shards of miles of mirrors
falling and cracking to perfect gardens.

I never inspect the withered assumption
of my face's petty dialogue in rain drops,
the deceptive spreading of the words
oozing from the skin to the edges of water
etched on the ground by gravity and wishing.

Passing for the seriousness of my eye,
platitudes of my white collar or
the perfect posture of my lips, it skirts
from the leaves of the plant hiding me
and sits stoic like stone in my pupil,
mute and unassuming, like Rashi.

To gather myself I will swim naked
in the wind, bending my blind elbows
in circles, stopping now to dance
like the cherubic gold on the ark,
and gather myself from the particles
of this excitement another structure,
one closely resembling the beginning.

The Model

Sometimes I would see laughter in a rock;
the turn of a lizard in shadow was gorgeous,
populations and Gorgons moved in clouds;
a sudden alto phrase came out of a brick,
moments in the road spoke to me
in passionate Russian that evoked Pushkin;
I would make it rain and suddenly
there was the anguish of the theatre,
as I made the synagogue bend in the shower;
birds danced on a plateau of spiralling air
like my sisters in their stocking feet,
my roads were long and lethargic like Tolstoy;
so the world convulsed, heaved, and told itself,
while I painted it from my mirror.

Musician with Violin

I make my greatest music in private,
as I listen to silence for a prelude,
watch the shifting parlance of shadows
for the incremental rise in pitch
of the voices, the infinite voices
that inhabit solitude like air,
and then I caress the belly and back,
position my heart on the finger-board,
set the bow to the strings perfectly,
and the voices sit back in awe,
with eyes devouring the intricate homily
pouring affection out of us in worship as soft
as affection or an angel's eyelid
brushing the cheek, no longer alone.

The Poet Mazin

I regret
the jingle of the cup
in my fingers,
my thinning eyes.
Night plays
a sonata on the glass,
rapping lightly
with moonrays
on the keyboard,
the bass thud
landing in the wood.
I regret words,
the half thought
resting in my lap,
drinking the liquor
sloshing from the cup,
the images moaning
from the pangs of creation,
startling the page.
A faraway landscape
grows in the colors
of the bottle, imitating life.
I regret life too
for lending itself to recreation,
sublimating sin.

The Painter to the Moon

Somewhere in the white tapestry of memory,
in the porous globe of thought piled on thought,
infinite portals dotting the soul's light,
I yield my palette to the birth of color.

My garland is wedded to the rising of the moon,
sustaining its glimmer from the lunar light,
while my vertebrae spin like a tube of curtain
wound around with its woven leaves and petals.

When the circle is full, my body forgets the ground,
flashes about in the moon's luminescence,
the clever trick of mirrors and fire,
while the world stops beneath me in finite form.

In my dreams color dwarfs any conception of it,
and, O Christ, my palette is some diviner,
spinning the world, breathing life's replications.

The Artist's Sister (Mania)

Blue omens hang in the window,
burning as if lit by hearts of gas;
night dims the carnations and leaves,
hangs them over with fingers pushing
their necks. Everyone is asleep
but you and your tortured hand going
from the water half-gone to the book
barely read or understood, the Torah.
Each night you leave the pears for
the visitant flying about in crystalline
splendor, another charlatan. I have been
meaning to tell you more of the power
of passion, of the body of lust
without thorns, but night keeps falling,
and day has me in the gay caprice of light,
a happy prisoner like the contented cormorant.

Listening to the Cock

His dominion over life and death is dissonant,
scattered and shoved about by his own
multiplying, the body that has swallowed
life itself and is pushed open by its fetus.

Above the crescent of the moon,
above the rootless upturned tree glistening
in night air, we sing from the swine's breast,
in harmony that denotes spring and denies death.

His crowing is aided by the violinist
plucking from his plumage, demanding
the submission of earth, of whisper and kiss,
of all the fuddling commotion of life.

Listening, we point the swine's hoofs
at his delusion, his seeming arrogance, his song,
the splintered shriek from his beak
and the imprisoned scrape of the violin's bow.

The Revolution

Men and guns are the dramaturgs of history,
pointing their smoking barrels and fingers,
educated by the enduring, incensed by hope,
setting their minds to the weaving of new flags
and the burning of old ones with their new dominions,
approaching the stage with bellies bursting
with food stolen from the privileged.
They assault the wisdom, the tradition
of longsuffering and liberation announced
by the Divine. A rabbi sighs and clutches
the Torah, a drunken soldier dying near his feet,
women and children desperately holding to his eyes
from poor rooftops, as the world is cut and chiseled.
The rabbi prays in the center of the stage,
God's prescience animates the audience of the mad.

The Soul of the City

Persecution and persecution--round the spirit
it entwines and attaches like a clinging vine
with no visible root and a crest and blossom
that obey the silent song piped from within.

I paint the withered body clad in the bloody cloth
with deft hands and divided heart, looking
past my own vision behind me to wingless spirits
appointed by the denial and splintered hope in the sky.

Suffering is only pointless if forgotten,
if the children do not hear the scraping blades
around them or the dirgeful call of the past,
if they are allowed to slip innocently into castigation.

My soul kindly advises what my eyes wildly declare,
the stark carpentry of the Cross, the hopeful
glancing upward at councils and patriarchs,
and the welcoming assurance of the past.

Peasant Life

When he leaves me at evening time,
I enter blue rooms dreaming above,
leaving the spare house and tattered life,
looking for freedom by stepping into
the glass of my own regret. Sometimes
in the morning, I watch his hat disappearing
down the walkway, the whip flapping
alongside his neck, threatening the fanciful
burst of laughter from stupid eyes in the trees,
and the longing comes out of my throat
like a vine with tears for leaves,
a vine that leaves my mouth and dances
in song through the house and out to my neighbors
who put their hands to their ears
to reassure themselves. Such loneliness is madness.

I and the Village

I come home with my scythe and sorrow,
my wife dances in the street to greet me;
all day stabbing the earth with this long knife,
slicing the stems of wheat until I hear them
crying in a golden choir that falls whimpering
in the sun; my wife has been pulling the teats
of the cow until the bucket fills, and the cow
glances at the sky, pleading with bulging sides;
the music of village chatter is low and dispersed;
the land has allowed us once more to rearrange,
to divide its spirit and quarter its heart
until the uniform heads of our food rise,
like a dominion of tutored children.

I do not know how long the silence will last,
the succumbing of the earth to our poking;
as no peace is equal; some heart goes away
tearful and wanting. For this I offer the cow
a bouquet of fruit and roses, that the earth
may see I am tired of beating it for sustenance,
that I miss the dance of my birth
and my innocent following the world —
not choking it with crude aspirations to divinity.

Wounded Soldier

A delectable silence comes over the guns,
fog doubles itself above the heads of trenches,
beating thin percussion when birds brave
the flipping corpses in mud struggling
to move back in the womb, move back
in the arms of a woman inviolate.

Suddenly I want a cup of tea and cake,
the tongue of a waitress I remember
who smiled and took away the empty cup,
and the soft shudder of her breasts bumping —
suddenly I want an exit from this compartment
of a train driving through my head, from this dream.

The rough mouths of the cannons
are like hungry miners waiting to belch
in the bistro, rubbing their black hands
until the nails are blackened thoroughly,
their faces beaten hard by the association
with stone, and every muscled movement
threatens violence, the violence of stone
hurtling through the air. Now silent,
now washed in the slicing tenor of rain
cutting the cannon's edge, like a piper
with his ability to hone and wear down,
the power of perpetual rain to obliterate,
to beat the tyranny of stone to non-being.

Through my sleep come three ushers,
limping along in disheveled uniforms,
and one is like me, clearer as they move on,
as I recognize first my face, then the scar
my brother gave me as a child; my voice
falls on my own deaf ears, and
I know I am in the only place where
voice and song must heed voice and song,
where every truth must fall back on itself
like a perfect epiphany dictating
its own portrait to empty spaces.

The train settles into its tracks,
its smooth skidding of steel on steel
strikingly absent, replaced by a requiem.

The Fall of Icarus

Testing your father's craft
until his ideas cracked under the weight
of your impudence, you plummeted
like a single feather, making lazy sways,
back and forth as you floated
down to earth, rejected by the sun.

The hecklers and mourners alike
stood beneath you, their feet safely
wedded to the earth, in obedience
to the authority of gravity and the divine
limitations of the human, safely
and softly placed where you must crash and break.

And in those quick moments as a feather,
you realized you could not have flight alone,
that you needed another host like you,
all guaranteed the song the air emits
when it consents to the wing,
when it elects to make the body ethereal.

You lapsed into your dream of a bird,
and, against earth's reclamation, were inviolate.

The Falling Angel

Departures from favor always halt
the music, stop the hand sliding the bow,
make the fingers on the strings arthritic,
until silence is mated with the smooth clock,
it's ticking going over the deadpan face
of the town while a single fire falls.

A single fire drawing a red line across
the moon, a voice that could awaken the dead,
now struggling to call out to figures of Christ,
to a rabbi clutching the Torah, a voice
sheared of its authority, struggling to cling
to any icon in the continuum of faith.

Her wings aflame, she wonders if, in Pandemonium,
some custom will greet her and she can sit
as she did in our houses and have her
ever capriccio cajoled and revered,
or will she be forced into the conspiracy,
to come back to us at night with evil sanction.

Falling, her eyes meet the eyes of the loving,
the pitying, the helpless. God's edict is obeyed.

The Pinch of Snuff

Minutes in meditation
tempt me to dashes
of it in my lips
to settle me on the word.

I keep a can
for the dark saliva
cogitation gives
after hours of study.

Some truth evades
the smell and lands
in my head,
taking root in vacant rooms.

Such a slovenly habit
should have been available
to Joshua as his knees
buckled before battle.

I am sworn to erudition,
resigned to the silent
marching of worlds
into my mind.

Such wisdom allows
a rabbi a pinch of snuff.

Jew at Prayer

If Solomon had my problems,
he would have driven his concubines
away into the hills, opened
his vaults to the poor and childless,
retreated to Moses' desert
to pray the still voice out of the sand,
in a robe torn and fetid with his sweat.

Women pour on me their suffering,
filling my spine like gravel crowding
a glass tube, likely to splinter
with one uncounted blast of my heart,
flickering over the Siddur as I reread
for the power that shoots between
word and act, voice and flesh.

A friend is coming tonight, after feeding.
We'll steal a cup of wine, put a sign
in the window. I am tired of visions.

Green Violinist

Some glass angel is summoned
by the flirting cries of my strings,
and another feeds me with music,
the soft sustaining by faith and nonchalance.

Everything halts when I play,
the slow drag of clouds colliding
becomes thick and heavy like stones
and mountains in the sky as my strings cry.

Men herald the sudden entry of music and angels
from their wagons and doorways,
waiting to kiss the floor of heaven
as it descends, while I hold time entranced.

A child sits and listens in an open window,
clapping the mating of violin and soul.

Purim

The wind receives gifts to the dead,
when they are busy about their endless chores,
instant appearances here and there,
darting pious eyes at a congregation
remembering the decree of a jubilant Mordecai
and the anxious bullets of the Russian spirit.

Their gifts are transfigured and accumulated,
piled high in a vast mausoleum,
reduced there to the size of a tear,
or the heart of a sigh, remembered
by a member of the host posted permanently,
watching over the intentions of men and women.

To the honored, announcements fly out,
horsemen ride the blue fabric of dreams,
apparitions dance above houses of the the poor,
young men shed their selfishness strangely,
hymns come to the mute hearts of the disconsolate.
Somewhere in their flights the dead see.

Cemetery Gates

Above the dead, a concerto plays,
in blue prisms as the sky disappears;
the strings silence themselves for the piano,
pianissimo, with the moon transforming,
turning to triangles of white settling
in the trees. The percussion
makes the dormant blood chortle,
under tombstones haunched above ground,
like steady shoulders and set heads,
as the strings return a whistling soprano
to the pillars of the gate, and living stone
is on the earth again, heating the words
inscribed in it, expanding in auras, speaking.
The Midrash is true. After life is life.